MICHAEL

CELEBRATION OF A CHAMPION

CAMPBELL

FOREWORD BY SIR BOB CHARLES
PREFACE BY MICHAEL CAMPBELL

MICHAEL
CELEBRATION OF A CHAMPION
CAMPBELL

MARTIN CROWE & CRAIG TIRIANA

REED

REED PUBLISHING (NZ) LTD
TE KARUHI TĀ TĀPUI O REED (AOTEAROA)
Established in 1907, Reed is New Zealand's largest
book publisher, with over 600 titles in print.
www.reed.co.nz

Published by Reed Books, a division of Reed Publishing (NZ) Ltd, 39 Rawene Road,
Birkenhead, Auckland 10. Associated companies, branches and representatives
throughout the world.

National Library of New Zealand Cataloguing-in-Publication Data
Crowe, Martin.
Michael Campbell : celebration of a champion / Martin Crowe
& Craig Tiriana. 1st ed.
ISBN-13: 978-0-7900-1085-4
ISBN-10: 0-7900-1085-2
1. Campbell, Michael, 1969-2. Golfers—New Zealand.
3. Golf—Tournaments. I. Tiriana, Craig. II. Title.
796.352092—dc 22

Paperback
ISBN-13: 978-0-7900-1085-4
ISBN-10: 0-7900-1085-2
Hardback
ISBN-13: 978-0-7900-1088-5
ISBN-10: 0-7900-1088-7

First published 2005
Project manager: Peter Dowling
Design by Jason Anscomb

Printed in New Zealand

Contents

Foreword

MICHAEL CAMPBELL first came to my attention in 1992 when, together with his team, he won the Eisenhower Trophy in Vancouver — a first for an amateur golf team from New Zealand.

Since then I have followed his golf career with interest.

After turning professional in 1993, he made headlines around the world by leading the 1995 Open Championship at St Andrews, before finishing equal third. Michael has won many tournaments around the world, but his crowning achievement has come in 2005 with his victory in the US Open Championship at Pinehurst, North Carolina.

Coming from a small country like New Zealand, this is a significant achievement. It is more so on this golf course, considered the greatest work of Donald Ross. I have played Pinehurst on many occasions, and can testify to just how difficult a golf course it is, particularly under United States Golf Association conditions.

I have had the privilege of playing golf with Michael on only a few occasions, but from also observing his swing on television it is no surprise to me that he has enjoyed the success that has come his way. From an early age he had the benefit of excellent tuition with sound fundamentals, moulding a swing of economy and precision. He has had his ups and downs through physical and mental interference, but when he gets into his stride he becomes a fierce competitor, and he has proved himself by having gone head to head with the greatest players of the day.

I wish Michael continued success in the greatest game of all and recommend this book to all who aspire to a dream of greatness.

SIR BOB CHARLES
Lytham, Oxford
New Zealand

Preface

HOWEVER LONG you may spend in a career of professional golf, nothing really prepares you for the walk down the 18th fairway at Pinehurst knowing you are a putt or two away from claiming one of golf's Major titles. Nothing can prepare you for the feeling when the final putt drops.

Winning a Major had always been a childhood dream of mine and the dream became reality at Pinehurst on Sunday 19 June. Pinehurst is a real haven of golf – the atmosphere really is extraordinary and it is an incredibly challenging course. Beyond that, I'd never fulfilled my potential in America. I'd been close in Major championships before and had won 13 tournaments as a professional, but success in the US Open was not something anyone was predicting when I was down to the wire during qualifying for the event.

To put it plainly, my form at the start of 2005 had been lousy – I had missed the cut in five straight tournaments. A lot of followers might have lost confidence in my ability to perform, but the one person who didn't lose confidence was me.

I didn't panic. At the start of the year I'd taken a look at what was important in my life, put my golf into perspective, and realised I needed to make some changes. I moved to a new management agency, IMG, and went full-time with my coach, Jonathan Yarwood. I also changed my sport psychologist and my physical trainer. Cambo Golf was an energised team and I knew we were going to get up.

What made the difference at the 2005 US Open? I had no expectation of my performance that week and it helped that the media didn't pay much attention to me until halfway through the final round. It also helped that I had the inner confidence due to my recent form, and didn't put undue pressure on myself. Ultimately, I knew that I was playing really well and ready to win a Major!

The fantastic support I receive from New Zealand has always spurred me on. Knowing that my family and friends, golf fans and non-golf fans alike, were crowded around TV sets back home cheering me on was a real boost. Being able to celebrate with the New Zealand fans afterwards (including, a nice surprise, Martin Crowe and Marcus Wheelhouse) made the victory even sweeter.

'Overwhelming' would be the best word to describe the reception I received when my family and I returned to New Zealand in July. From the Prime Minister to the school kids in Titahi Bay, everyone was genuinely ecstatic about my victory, which means a lot to me.

I've said before that I'd like my legacy to be that of inspiring young Kiwis to come through into the top ranks of world golf. During my trips home to New Zealand I want to work on encouraging our young golfers to take up the game and reach their potential. For now, winning more tournaments is the best way to inspire them.

And so far, so good. I'm hungry to win more prestigious tournaments, and the World Match Play title in September proved that the US Open was no one-off. Needless to say I want to win more Major championships and I hope that in reading this book you can share some of the magic of those unforgettable days and memories at Pinehurst, North Carolina.

Kia ora tatou.

Michael Campbell
November 2005

'The chosen one.'

Cambo's win at Pinehurst

MARTIN CROWE

Throughout his illustrious career, the greatest of them all, Jack Nicklaus, would often say, 'You don't choose to win the US Open; the US Open chooses you.'

It is true that the US Open is the toughest test of golf in all the Majors. Every year, players try their best to not give up par over four gruelling rounds.

Competing for the second Major of the year in 2005 were the Big 5: Tiger Woods, Vijay Singh, Ernie Els, Phil Mickelson and Retief Goosen, the reigning US Open champion.

Two months earlier Tiger had triumphed again at the US Masters for his fourth Green Jacket and looked hungry to chase the Grand Slam.

The field was deemed to be as strong as the days when Palmer, Nicklaus, Player and Trevino reigned supreme. The course was regarded as one of the best around, the test as brutal as it could be. All the ingredients were there to make this as memorable as any Major.

The 105th US Open Championship was always going to be a week of high drama, fever-pitch emotions and immense challenges. The one to win would indeed be, as Jack would say, 'the chosen one'.

Pinehurst is a naturally beautiful little settlement. Set amongst pine forests in North Carolina in the United States, it's a tiny spot in a large country, just a drop in the ocean, but it is Mecca when it comes to golf. As you drive through the towering pines you feel uplifted and a little different; a kind of spiritual feeling emerges. It's a pretty special place. For golf lovers it's an institution.

Less than a kilometre from the lovely town centre is the famous No 2 course, designed and developed by the Scottish immigrant Donald Ross, and the second of eight outstanding golf courses at Pinehurst. For a century now, it has been an icon of golf-course design in the United States.

When the name 'Pinehurst No 2' is mentioned, it is done so with a hint of awe, a mark of the enormous respect it has earned.

Everyone you talk to says that to conquer Pinehurst No 2 you need strength of character, emotional control, an abundance of talent and, most of all, a spirit to fight the toughest yet fairest test of all. Actually, the real honest ones just say it's 'bloody brutal'.

The man who always seemed to embody that spirit and character was Payne Stewart. He won here on an emotionally charged Sunday in June back in 1999, and his win was made more poignant when he was tragically killed in a plane crash just months later.

So as you walk down the drive towards Donald Ross' masterpiece, the memory of Payne's victory dance on the 18th is the very thing that hits you first. Flags depicting that highly charged moment were fluttering every 10 paces.

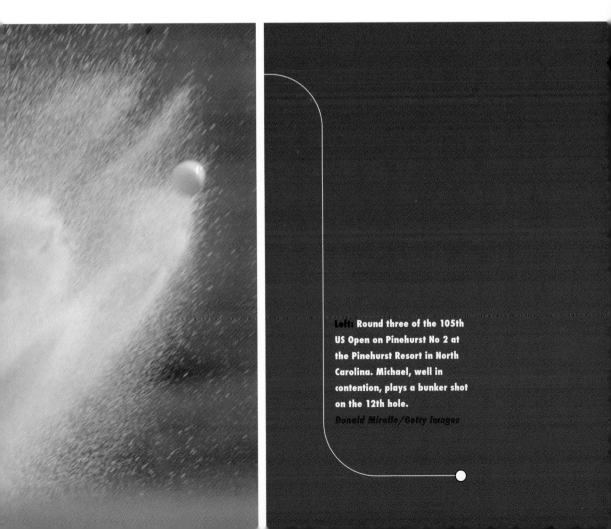

Left: Round three of the 105th US Open on Pinehurst No 2 at the Pinehurst Resort in North Carolina. Michael, well in contention, plays a bunker shot on the 12th hole.
Donald Miralle/Getty Images

For Michael Campbell, his life and destiny had always been golf. Not surprisingly, he is of Scottish heritage and the connections with Scotland throughout his career have been notable.

Born near the beautiful Mt Taranaki, Michael spent a lot of his first five years with his grandparents on their farm near Patea in Taranaki. When Michael was four years old, his grandmother Titihuia told him he would change people's lives.

Since he made his first swing at the age of seven at the Titahi Bay Golf Club, he has oozed natural talent. In his early years the rolling hills and the sea breeze of the Kapiti Coast and Titahi Bay provided challenging conditions in which to learn to play golf. It was seriously good conditioning.

Twenty years later Michael would lead arguably the most glorious Major of them all, The Open Championship at St Andrews, a course as vulnerable to the elements as the one at Titahi Bay. Going into the final round of The 1995 Open Championship with a two-shot lead, he stumbled and missed, but he did not fall. He just learnt a really tough lesson.

Straight away he confirmed his goal of wanting to win a Major. If he could, he would not only change his own life forever, he would inspire many others to reach out and go higher too. Titihuia was right. He would change people's lives.

It had been a long journey, but he was destined to get there.

When Cambo arrived at Pinehurst, deep inside he felt nearly ready. The year had not gone smoothly, and he had missed the cut on five occasions.

So he made some changes, as he explained in an interview with Sky Sport in early August: 'At the start of the year I changed the whole dynamics of Cambo Golf. I signed on my coach full-time; I changed my sport psychologist, my chiropractor, because it wasn't working. If things don't work, you've gotta change. I had a bit of a rough start, but I was close to playing well, and during that time I was emailing people saying, "Hey, don't panic, everything is fine." I could feel a greatness coming. Six weeks out from Pinehurst I started to play well.'

He had qualified for the Championship by shooting 68–71 at Walton Heath Golf Club (on the Old and New courses respectively) in Surrey a month earlier, in a very strong field that would offer only nine qualifying spots. It was the first time in US Open history that two qualifying events were held overseas. On a traditional old heathland course Cambo played the two rounds on one day, a Monday.

Exhausted from a long drive after finishing The Celtic Manor Wales Open the previous day, he played beautifully for 4 under for the first round and looked a comfortable qualifier. Fatigue set in for the second round. However, Cambo found some inner strength and made a late rally, finishing by sinking a 5-foot putt for birdie on the final hole to take the last spot and avoid a play off. This was a gutsy display and proved to Cambo himself that he was on the right track. He was in another Major, and he would, after all, make at least one trip to the United States in 2005.

For years Cambo had crossed the Atlantic only to fall short and miss the cut, almost without exception. He was uncomfortable with the environment and the lifestyle, and try as he might he never felt at ease or inspired. His confidence was low when he played in the US.

Arriving on the Sunday night prior to the week of the US Open, Cambo checked into the Pine Needles Lodge. He was alone. His caddie, Mike Waite, went up the road to join six other caddies in a rented house.

Jonathan Yarwood, his coach, arrived on Monday afternoon from Florida. He would stay two nights before heading back south to be with his expectant wife.

On Monday morning Cambo played a practice round with friends Vijay Singh and Paul McGinley. Vijay noticed something in Cambo's bunker play and gave him a tip. Heavens above, what a tip it proved to be!

Left: Campbell pitches onto the green during the US Open qualifier at Walton Heath Golf Club, England. By mid-2005 Michael's game was re-energised and refocused, and had shown steady improvement. In June, the USGA held two qualifying events for the US Open offshore for the first time, offering just nine qualifying spots in the UK. Michael snaffled one, not realising he was buying a ticket to greatness.
Richard Heathcote/Getty Images

17

Cambo was getting desperate to find his putting touch again and had reverted to the belly putter for the first time. While his long game was impeccable, his putting was off the mark. He'd lost his feel. He had thought one final change was needed. It wasn't. Yarwood told him to throw the belly putter away. Trusting his coach once again, he did.

Yarwood: 'Viewing Cambo's stats and spending a few of the previous weeks with him at the preceding events, I felt that his ball striking was bearing the fruit of the swing work we had done. He had had some top ten finishes in previous events but his putting was letting him down, which belied the fact that he was flushing the ball like Cambo can. We both said to each other that those weeks prior, despite having good finishes, were the worst scores he could have shot.

'I nearly fell over when he whipped a belly putter out. I discussed with him that this is the last resort to players who have never had a good touch on the greens. I said he had always had that touch, and got him to understand that it was just a temporary glitch and he did not need to panic and go to such extremes.'

Cambo: 'The most important thing we worked on was technique. If your technique is correct, it will free up the mind. After I could see on video that my technique was pretty good we then worked on pace. We had a real good plan about my putting.'

All afternoon, on their own at the Pine Needles golf course, they practised putting. They went through the basics, then once they were locked in and programmed, they started to work on feel and speed. In particular, he concentrated on 40-foot putts. Then 6-foot putts. Finally, after five hours of intense practice and tutelage, he put his Odyssey putter down.

18

Right: A solid performance over two rounds on one day was capped by a final-hole birdie on the New Course to enable Campbell to qualify at Walton Heath, Surrey, in June. *Mark Bass*

Yarwood: 'We changed about nine things in his address to create a foundation that would allow the putter to open and close as it should on a slight arc back and through. The ball immediately started on line, with the correct launch and end-over-end roll. But more importantly, it clicked with him!

'Lastly we did work with his eyes closed for his long-distance speed control. Everything clicked in like a dream. Being away from the tournament venue helped as we had no crowds and we could do some good filming. After that, the camera was put away. Some quick tightening of his swing, some new shots around the green like a 3 wood up the banks surrounding the greens, standing closer to his chips to nip them better, and he was ready to go!'

Tuesday was a practice round, a strategy and planning day. They would walk and play the course and work out the game plan.

There was no doubt whatsoever that every part of his game was going to be tested this week. Driving was a premium for a start. Changing his driver earlier in the year to a new Callaway Fusion FT3 had been critical. His length and accuracy had improved out of sight. It had to be sharp for Pinehurst No 2. If you hit the rough, it was so brutal that only the very strongest physically would have a chance to blast out.

Which brings up another key for Cambo. *He is really fit.*

Then came the challenge of hitting the greens. Every hole, with the exception of the par-5 4th, had a green that bore resemblance to an upside-down saucer. The area of green throughout the 18 holes that was regarded safe to hit and stay on was just 28 per cent. The other 72 per cent would not hold the ball on the green. Approach shots to each hole required pinpoint accuracy, and that had nothing to do with the position of the pin. Sometimes just staying on the green, even with a 40-footer to go, was deemed a success.

If you missed the green, you faced the greatest test of your imagination to scramble up and down. Many choices came into play: a 3 wood, a

wedge, a putter; whatever got the ball rolling up and on to the green at a speed that would hold.

Par was a great score. Talk around the traps on Tuesday had some players like Phil Mickelson and John Daly predicting that 7 to 8 over could win the tournament. Cambo thought 2 or 3 over might be enough.

Wednesday dawned and so did the searing heat. Temperatures of 40°C with high humidity forced most competitors to early-morning practice and little else. Tiger Woods only played the front nine at 6.30 am and his final preparation was done and dusted by 10.30 am. He took to the shower and a cool afternoon in the shade.

Left: Searing temperatures, intense media focus and high tension marked the build-up to the start of the US Open on 13 June at Pinehurst. But Campbell stayed cool and calm. Here he tees off on the 12th hole during a practice round.
Ross Kinnaird/Getty Images

By the end of Wednesday Yarwood was satisfied with his star pupil's prep and declared it time to leave. His wife was due. So was Cambo.

Interestingly, throughout the week Cambo was unreachable by phone. He had left his mobile somewhere back in England and the only people that could get through to him were his wife, Julie and his coach, Yarwood. It would seem that accidentally he couldn't be contacted and therefore potentially distracted. Instead he was allowed to just think about and imagine playing golf. His nightly chats with Jonathan helped too.

Yarwood: 'We talked each night on the phone. All along I was trying to play down the enormity of the event. I would say things like "It is only like any other event, it has 18 greens and 18 tees like any other. The media make it different, don't get sucked in. Follow your process that got you here. Prepare well, execute your plan, and the outcome will take care of itself." We talked a lot about the process taking care of the outcome. It helped keep him in the present and not get too far ahead of himself.

'As he rose up the leaderboard through the week, I would tell him things to deflect the fear of failure. Things like "No matter what, it is great experience under your belt, you have nothing to lose, no one is watching you as they think you do not have a chance." Little things to defuse the situation, laced with things that might fire him up a touch!'

At his last Major outing, Cambo had had a contingent of 12 people around him. All that seemed to do was drain him of his energy and detract from his focus. Now on the eve of the toughest test of golf on offer it was just Michael and Mike. The golfer and the caddie. Two Taranaki-born lads, Michael from Hawera and Mike from Stratford, with a clear purpose.

Right: Round two, 17 June, and Michael follows the progress of his tee shot on the 15th tee. After a solid, comfortable first round, Campbell could well have faltered. But his calmness and assuredness continued as he shot a one under par 69, with six birdies, to climb up the leaderboard into sixth-equal slot.
Jamie Squire/Getty Images

Mike's job was to keep Cambo in check, keep him in the present. To keep him focused on the next shot and to distract him from dwelling on and judging the past minutes' performance or future consequences was crucial.

The caddie's role cannot be underestimated. In Mike, Cambo had a mate who could read him quickly, speak to him honestly and get him to the next shot, the next swing immediately.

They set off together.

The first round proved fruitful. Starting out on the back nine, he began with three solid pars, turning round at even par. The front nine was more adventurous with birdies at 4 and 8 but bogeys at 2, 6 and 7 resulting in a round of 71, one over par, four shots behind the leaders Olin Browne and Rocco Mediate. Overall, Cambo drove it well, putted great, hung in when he needed to, and felt calm throughout. He was feeling a little different.

Cambo: 'Funnily enough, I felt really comfortable. Normally at a Major championship you see all these grandstands, and all these people, but this time I just felt comfortable, for what reason I'm not sure.'

The first round saw some of the best already out of the tournament: Davis Love III, Justin Leonard and Kenny Perry to name a few. Cambo needed to consolidate his first round with a steady, consistent repeat performance. If he did, he would make a cut that was long overdue in a Major, let alone in a tournament in the US.

Instead of grafting to survive the cut, he found an extra calmness and touch to shoot 69, 1 under par, including six birdies. He birdied both the par fives, the 4th and the 10th, as well as the 13th again. Significantly, he nailed the difficult par-3 17th, a hole that was to give him fond memories. He made the cut comfortably at level par and settled in nicely in 6th position, two shots behind leaders Browne, Goosen and Jason Gore.

Cambo: 'Last time I made the cut in the US Open was back in 2000 at Pebble Beach when Tiger won. For some reason, I had this thing in my mind about America and not playing too well and finally I said, "Enough of this, cut those cables about negativity about America. I've had enough of this bullshit! Let's go and play well."'

For the third round Cambo was paired with Australian Mark Hensby, on what is often referred to as 'moving day'. The trouble at Pinehurst No 2 was that generally the only direction you move was backwards. Staying put was perfect.

They teed off in the third-to-last group mid-afternoon, with the temperature at its hottest and the wind swirling in the trees. Conditions were at their toughest. There would be few survivors on this Saturday.

Cambo birdied the first and moved to within one of the lead. But despite scrambling par on the toughest hole on the course, the 2nd, he faltered over the next four holes, dropping three shots, to fall back to 2 over.

Pars were the absolute key. Staying still on the leaderboard was a worthy goal. Just hang in and graft on each and every shot. Be patient, and wait for an opening.

Cambo had found the required patience and the ability to stay in the 'now' during the week, and it was at this point he found it again. He parred 7 and 8 and through this steady period he did find an opening and birdied the difficult par-3 9th. From there it was plain sailing through the back nine, other than a bogey on the 11th. Solid striking, sensible strategy, superb speed on the greens.

Then the moment came that defined the first three rounds. Playing the par-3 17th, Cambo, trying to cut a 7 iron towards a right pin, overplayed it and hit the right trap. He had short-sided himself and now had almost no chance to get close with the pin just 5 yards away and all downhill.

Then he remembered Vijay's bunker tip.

Cambo: 'On that Monday when I played with Vijay, he taught me this certain shot 'cause I was cutting across the ball and getting too much spin, instead of flopping it up high and letting it roll out with less spin. So he gave me the tip and showed me how to do it.

'Then on the Saturday at 17 I thought I'd do the "Vijay shot".

'It went in and everyone went ballistic. I was pumped and I turned around to Mike. He was emotionless so I said, "What's your problem?" He said, "Good shot, but you've got the last hole to play, so hit your

Right: Viva le 'Vijay shot'! Campbell is elated after holing out for birdie on the 17th green during a decisive period in round three. Earlier in the week during practice, Vijay Singh had shown him how to play from a semi-buried lie in the sand with less spin. It worked to perfection.
Streeter Lecka/Getty Images

tee shot." "Hey, that's great," I said, "thanks for getting me back to the now."

'Mike can read me like a book, and he's a real asset to my game.'

Cambo finished only 1 over for the round and the tournament and moved into the top four with Goosen 4 shots ahead at 3 under, while Americans Gore and Browne were at even par. 'The Goose', the reigning champion after his ice-cool win at Shinnecock Hills the previous year, stood as red-hot favourite. Tiger was prowling, but growling, 6 back.

Cambo went back to the Lodge for his usual routine. Salmon and vegies for dinner, two glasses of red wine. It was the same routine almost the whole week. Quietly enjoying the company of a couple of fellow competitors, he was purely and utterly focused on, yet relaxed about, his golf and nothing else.

He would tee off at 2.50 pm on Sunday 19 June, with Olin Browne, the penultimate pairing. But what did he do until the tee time?

Cambo: 'I got up at 7.30 am and read for two hours. Then I ate a slow breakfast. Then I headed to the course and stretched out. Then with an hour and a half to go, I had lunch with Goose and then some practice and a putt. Easy routine, mate.'

Cambo enjoyed the fact that he wasn't being talked about going into the final day. Ten years previously he had a two-shot lead at St Andrews, but the tension and anxiety was too great. Now, he just felt at ease. Would the Goose win again, or could big Jason Gore continue the fairytale? Or would Tiger charge as he always did? Then there was Sergio Garcia, and Vijay as well.

The experts discarded both Browne and Campbell. Their storyline didn't fit for the romantics. Browne, a journeyman; Campbell, a Kiwi lad. Ho hum, they said.

So come 2.50 pm Cambo pulled out his 3 wood and hit a nice fade down the left, ending the perfect distance for a 'little' 9 iron. It was just part of the strategy. Hit it too close to the green and it's a harder shot. Nice start for the Kiwi lad.

Above: Campbell allows himself the luxury of celebrating his birdie on the 17th green during round three, but caddie Michael Waite quickly brought him back to earth, ready to focus on his next tee shot. Campbell was learning to let go of shots just played and not contemplate the ones too far ahead.
Jim Watson/AFP/Getty Images

29

Of the final six groups only three players hit the fairway on the first hole. Of the final six groups only Cambo birdied; most bogeyed, including Tiger.

Five Kiwis, including Marcus Wheelhouse and I, were identified in the crowd on this day. Ray McLean, a 60-year-old car dealer from Christchurch, joined us early in the piece and the three of us together walked stride for stride with our man.

As we moved off to see Cambo play the 2nd hole, no one came with us. The crowd either had gone off with Tiger two groups ahead, or were staying to watch Goosen and Gore. From that moment until the 16th, if you were a Cambo follower you had the most perfect view of every shot he would play.

Cambo's first hiccup came off the tee on the par 4 5th hole. He pulled it left and found deep, deep rough. After a debate with Mike about which shot to play, he took his caddie's advice and courageously blasted out to the fairway.

The next shot set the tone for the day. It was 48 yards to a left pin, perched on a ledge with trouble everywhere except a square 2-yard area to the right of the pin. The 5th hole, the second-hardest hole, was proving to be Cambo's toughest challenge during the week with bogeys on two of the first three rounds.

Right: Acknowledging the warm reception of the gallery on the 5th green during the final round on 19 June. Michael felt at ease: there was no pressure on him, no expectation he'd win. He could play his own game while the crowd chased Tiger Woods up ahead or Jason Gore and Retief Goosen in the following group.
Ross Kinnaird/Getty Images

His pitch was struck crisply and it spun miraculously to a yard to the right of the pin. The crowd, on seeing the ball check, let out a groan of massive respect and awe. Five minutes later, after the putt was negotiated, Michael Campbell led the US Open.

Cambo: 'I couldn't believe it to be honest, 'cause I was playing for second. Goose had won the US Open twice before and all of a sudden he's off to a bad start. I can't control what he does; all I can do is do my best and hang in. Then I'm leading and I quickly got used to the feeling.'

By the 8th it was clear he was the only one with a game under control. No mistakes on the scorecard, while around him there was carnage and chaos. Goosen, Gore and Browne had combined to record 17 dropped shots at the turn. It was astonishing, but it was also Pinehurst No 2. If Goosen felt his nerve collapse, that was confirmation that this was truly the toughest test of all.

Cambo was holding firm, and despite another pull off the tee on 8, he recovered to leave only a 3-footer for par. Surprisingly, he missed the downhill slider and for the first time the crowd sensed that Cambo might start backing up to the others.

Cambo: 'I was cool, to be honest. Big deal, so what, it's only a game. Just move on to the next one, simple as that. I got rid of the shot very, very quickly. For me it's quite unusual, I usually cling on too long, but once again I cut those cables and moved on to the next shot.'

Despite that view, Cambo hit a poor 7 iron three minutes later to the par 3 9th hole and faced an unlikely up and down from his position below the green. He took out his putter then replaced it with his 3 wood. The pin was 17 yards away, a couple of yards above the level of the ball.

Cambo: 'I tell you what, that was an unbelievable shot I played, using my 3 wood to bump it up the hill. It's hard to explain; you can't tell on TV how tough it is. The turf round the green is very bumpy and the putter makes it jump too much so the 3 wood gets it rolling better.'

The 2-foot putt for par was achieved and Cambo strode to the start of his final-round back nine with a 1-shot lead over Goosen, playing one hole back, and 2 over Woods, a hole ahead.

Traditionally, the start of the back nine on the Sunday of a Major is where the tournament finds another gear. Now, the challenge is all mental; it's all about nerve and who can hold it.

Clearly Goosen's nerve had deserted him on this day. The only challenger therefore would come from arguably the greatest golfing talent ever, Tiger Woods.

As Cambo drove long and true up 10, Tiger sunk a 3-footer on 11, to register back-to-back birdies. Cambo's lead for a few minutes was just a single stroke.

What started now summed up the mental toughness required for winning Majors. Tiger would strike a blow, and Cambo would immediately respond in emphatic fashion. So Cambo's response on 10 was to pitch to 25 feet and drain the difficult birdie putt. His putting now seemed to flow like a river.

He could see the line, track it to the hole and then, with his trust in technique secure, would let go mentally and instinctively find a way to get the ball in the hole. Two-shot lead again.

Right: In the final round, with Michael leading by a single stroke, by hole 10 it was a contest of stamina and mental strength between Tiger Woods and Campbell, with Tiger closing fast. With a majestic touch, Campbell holed a 25-foot putt for birdie. He was in the zone, in the 'now'.
David Cannon/Getty Images

A hush presided as a lightning warning was posted around the course. All the grandstands were emptied. Eerily, it was like the golfers were playing to no one.

Tiger parred the next three holes, quietly. Cambo, subconsciously needing another challenge from Tiger, now got overconfident and made a mistake on 11.

With 162 yards to the pin, Mike called for a 9 iron, centre of the green. Cambo disagreed. Feeling the wind swirling, he grabbed his wedge. Mike disagreed. Cambo backed off and had another think. He stayed with the wedge. Mike finally said, 'Okay, hit it right centre then.' Right centre would take bogey out of play, but possibly birdie too. Cambo swung hard and the ball went too straight, came up short and spun back into a deep sand trap. To his credit and acute instinct, he immediately apologised to Mike and laughed at his stupidity. He replaced a negative with a positive.

With his focus back in place, he called on Vijay's tip once again. The shot was delicate and required a cool touch. The ball came out soft and hit the top of the bank, rolled forward and just passed the hole to finish within 4 feet.

What we were witnessing here was a different Michael Campbell. Gone were the over-reactive responses to a mistake. In was a calmness and spirit that guided him back into the 'now'. It felt, amid the swaying pines of Pinehurst, like someone was watching over him, guiding him.

On 12, Cambo swung a 6 iron for his second shot from the semi rough. On impact he called out 'Oh no, it's come out so soft.' It appeared the ball would therefore come up short. Instead it kicked forward onto the green and ran to within 25 feet below the hole. It was karma.

Left: By the end of the 12th hole, the game had changed. It had become apparent that Tiger might not catch Campbell, and that Michael wasn't faltering as a perfect birdie putt proved. In fact, by the time he teed off on the 13th hole, his game was flowing superbly.
Ross Kinnaird/Getty Images

Saying no more, he turned and ran to the public toilet area. Naturally, all those watching thought the comfort stop was a result of plenty of drinking through another humid day. No one except Cambo and Mike knew that Cambo did something else. In the unpleasant environment of a smelly Port-a-loo, Cambo did 45 seconds of eye exercises!

Cambo: 'I had my eyes tested four months ago, because I was seeing putts the wrong way. All these tests were done on me and they gave me some eye exercises to do. It was explained it's like going to the gym; you train your muscles. Same thing with the eyes, you wake up in the morning and your eyes are a bit lazy, so they gave me these exercises to do.

'I couldn't do them in front of millions of people on the course so I ran off to the Port-a-loo to do my eye exercises. I could feel my body getting tired, my legs were aching, my eyes were sore, and I could sense tiredness creeping in.

'So as soon as I hit my shot on 12 I ran to the loo. I then grabbed my tee, moved it around in a circular motion and tried to watch the tip of the tee. After a while you can feel the muscles around the eyes straining and getting exercised and realigned properly.'

Amazing.

With his eyes rejuvenated Cambo dropped a perfect putt into darkness and Pinehurst No 2 came alive once and for all. Now it was 'game on'. Cambo wasn't going anywhere stupid after all. Tiger wasn't charging and the fans were starting to murmur: 'Who is this guy Campbell?'

For me, as a sportsman and loving the heat of any battle, I was now in sporting heaven. This was pure magic unfolding. Not only was it a privilege to be walking the fairways of one of America's greatest golfing venues, but also to see a fellow New Zealander on the path to victory was quite mesmerising.

Now, the pace of the whole event quickened. Now, we sensed people were starting to move more swiftly into position. Before we knew it, we were running for prime spots ourselves to watch the action unfold.

As Cambo's putt rolled in on 12, the lightning warning was removed and everyone filed back into the stands. The only lightning now was coming from the 'Kia Kaha' man. The strong man.

Pars for Tiger at 14 and Cambo at 13. The lead still 2 shots. Then another significant moment. Another example of why a Major is so dramatic. As Cambo stepped up to hit his 7 iron second shot into 14, a roar screamed from 15. Tiger had sunk a 6-footer for birdie. The pumped fists and steely eyes of the Tiger were in full evidence. Uh, oh.

Cambo backed off his approach shot, looked to 15 and nodded his approval. The Tiger was calling and Cambo acknowledged the challenge. The response was swift. Cambo stepped up and swung the club. It was another stunning shot. As the ball rolled gently past the hole to within 5 feet, Cambo turned again to 15 and doffed his cap. Cool, classy and in control.

And so it proved. That shot by Cambo into 14 was, for all intents and purposes, the killer punch. From there Tiger stumbled, and then fell, with bogeys on 16 and 17. Uncharacteristically, the world's best player went down for the count.

It came down now to one man. It came down to whether Michael Campbell could erase the demons of St Andrews 10 years ago. It came down to one man holding his nerve. It came down to his karma and his spirit rising to the surface.

It came down to destiny.

He played the last four holes so masterfully, despite enormous pressure, that he surely was being given a hand by the gods.

It was that good.

A mistake on the par-3 15th off the tee was easily corrected by a stupendous bunker shot. A pulled drive on 16 was corrected by taking some medicine, a fair bogey, and moving on.

Right: Campbell was playing like a master over the last few holes, and a glitch on the 15th was remedied by an outrageously deft shot out of a sand trap onto the green to six feet. As Michael said: 'If I went back there and played 10 shots from the same place, I wouldn't get close to that hole.'
Roberto Schmidt/AFP/Getty Images

Cambo: 'You have no idea how difficult that bunker shot on 15 was. If I went back there and played ten shots from the same place, I wouldn't get close to that hole. As I walked up to the bunker and saw my ball I said, "Oh no, this is going to be tough." I believe the toughest shot in golf is the 20-yard bunker shot. But Vijay had showed me the way to play it. By the time I got over the ball I got comfortable again.'

Then came the crème de la crème.

I stood behind the 17th tee, and saw the gloriously beautiful par 3 — 198 yards long, surrounded by bunkers, trees and grandstands. This was heavenly.

I could hear Mike tell Cambo, 'Long is dead. You're pumped, so it's an 8 iron. Hit it as hard as you like.'

What he was saying was an 8 iron would carry you over the bunker onto the green 179 yards away; 8 iron can't possibly go long and finish dead and allow a probable double bogey. Even coming up short of the green, or being bunkered, was better than long.

Cambo thought 7 iron. The distance suggested that. But he said nothing and, unlike at the 11th hole, he went with Mike's call.

Why he didn't question it could be this. He was now in a spiritual uplift. He was 'in the zone', and all his conditioning as a golfer, all his knowledge, all his support, all his instinct, was now working as 'one'.

As he hit that 8 iron I honestly thought I had never seen a more beautiful thing in sport. The sound off the club was pure magic. The hush around the entire hole was eerie and surreal. It was a moment I will never forget.

The way the ball floated and hung in the air, and then landed sweetly on the front of the green and rolled serenely to within 20 feet of the hole, was like it was all in slow motion. I shook my head in disbelief that I was being privileged to watch this moment.

Then I looked back to see Cambo rush off again to the toilets. Just one more time for good luck, he must have thought. A quick session on the eye exercises with his circling tee in front of his face and he was ready to face the music of a 20-footer uphill and a 3-shot lead with one to play.

Again, after hearing Tiger had birdied 18 to pull within 2 shots, Cambo replied sensationally. After refocusing his eyes, he sunk a magical putt.

Right: Michael hits his second shot on the 16th hole. While Tiger had bogeys on 16 and 17, Campbell held fast to his lead with magical putting. *Streeter Lecka/Getty Images*

Under the circumstances we were witnessing a perfect performance. Despite the odd mistake, which was only to be expected in this tricky neighbourhood, Cambo just answered every single goddamn challenge. It was merciless, outrageous, and yet undeniable.

Why did he win? Was it a fluke, as some locals would suggest? Absolutely not. Cambo was a seasoned campaigner. A pro since 1993, he had built up a reputation as being as skilful as any player on any given day. He'd beaten Tiger before and had chalked up 13 professional wins worldwide.

This was no novice out there. Cambo proved on the toughest course that he was definitely not an 80th world-ranked player, but a top 10 contender. He was potentially a modern-day great, up there with the Big 5. This win and the way he won made you believe that this was just the beginning.

Right: Yes! The last hole of the final round of the 105th US Open, on one of the world's toughest courses. With a few shots to spare, Campbell just had to get the job done sweetly.
Jamie Squire/Getty Images

He walked the 18th a true Major champion. He had a cushion and he was smart coming in. He got the job done.

On that airy final afternoon among those tall pines he heard his calling. He heard his grandmother Titihuia. He heard his whanau. He heard Bob Charles. Most of all, he heard the next generation of young New Zealanders calling for him to go higher. To come home.

As it dawned on him walking up the final hole that he had answered his calling, he turned to acknowledge his caddie, Mike. In return, with a tear in his eye, Mike simply said, 'This is why I caddie, Michael.'

There was one more interesting, unnerving fact. When he pitched out of the rough with his second shot, he had 77 yards left to the flag. This was exactly the same distance that Payne Stewart had had for his third shot, back on a similar afternoon in 1999. Cambo won with even par. The same as Payne.

Payne Stewart was guiding Cambo home too. The final putt went in and Cambo reached for the heavens. Then he covered his eyes for a moment with his cap.

Cambo: 'Holy shit, what have I done? I thought of my ancestors before me and then I looked within and I was searching around for all my emotions and the one that really stood out was "Holy shit, what have I done?"'

Above: Filled with the emotion of the moment and the enormity
of his achievement, Michael first looked skyward then briefly
buried his face in his cap. Twelve years in the professional
arena, including some years of terrible lows, had led to this: he
had answered his calling and climbed the mountain.
Donald Miralle/Getty Images

Fellow Kiwi Steve Williams, Tiger's caddie, greeted Cambo as he walked off the 18th. That added up to three Kiwis out of four in the two camps. They embraced and Steve said that this brief moment was the greatest sporting moment for New Zealand.

Two other Kiwis, Marcus Wheelhouse and I, watched our fellow countryman lift the glorious trophy up in the presentation that followed his final 2-foot putt for victory on the 18th green. With no mobile phone to call later, how were we going to finally reach him to say, 'You bloody beauty!'? As he walked off the green with the trophy, I barged past security with Marcus at my heels. Within seconds we were behind him as he began to walk down the steps to the changing rooms. 'Cambo, Cambo!' I yelled.

Right: 'This is why I caddie, Michael,' Mike Waite had said to Campbell as they neared the final green. The two have forged a close friendship and an excellent on-course partnership, and the results have flowed.
Jamie Squire/Getty Images

He turned, and seeing it was two Kiwis who had called, threw himself up the steps in a single bound and gave us the biggest bear hug of all time. He was in tears; he was rapt to see his own kind.

He whispered into Marcus' ear, 'Mate, 10 o'clock, Pine Needles Resort. See you there.'

We arrived at 9 pm and settled into a few beers and a feed. We met the pub owner and he couldn't get enough of us given we were Kiwis and he was putting up the US Open champion in his own pub.

At 9.50 Mike arrived and ordered 'Beer!' After Cambo had fulfilled his duties at the post-event press conference and with numerous photographers, and then made phone calls to Julie and the boys in England as well as family and press back home in New Zealand, at 10.08 pm Cambo arrived with the trophy, followed by more photographers.

He ordered 'Champagne! Dom Perignon'. He filled the trophy, took a long swig, and gave it to his best mate, Mike.

Right: Campbell is embraced by Steve Williams, caddie for Tiger Woods, on the 18th green. Williams called Michael's win one of the greatest moments in New Zealand sport. There were three Kiwis on the green that day: Campbell, Waite and Williams.
David Cannon/Getty Images

Over the next three hours everyone in the bar that night was allowed to drink out of the trophy. Some like Marcus and I went back for more and more and more. I smoked three big fat cigars during that time as well.

At 2 am the bar cleared somewhat. Left were five Kiwis. Cambo downed another beer, grabbed his trophy and went into a corner to sit down, alone.

He had seen a TV was on, and that a news bulletin had begun. He watched the newsreader announce that a Kiwi called Michael Campbell had won the US Open. Cambo shook his head. After a quiet minute or two, he turned to us and said, 'Hey, can you believe it?'

We acknowledged we couldn't. He held up the trophy one more time. 'It's true.' And it hit him like a thunderbolt. He *was* the US Open Champion. Forever, that's what he would be.

The Chosen One.

Left: Martin Crowe, Marcus Wheelhouse and other Kiwis helped their fellow countryman celebrate the victory at Pine Needles Resort. Michael ordered champagne for a well-deserved drink from the trophy, something most in the bar managed that night.
Martin Crowe

Above: The sweet taste of success. Michael kisses the trophy after becoming the 23rd international to have won the 105-year-old US Open title, and clinching the first Major win by a Kiwi since Sir Bob Charles won The Open Championship 42 years earlier.
Andy Lyons/Getty Images

Michael Campbell: Champion

CRAIG TIRIANA

Kia Kaha Ra

Kia kaha ra e tame e	Be strong, my grandson
Kia mau tonu te matauranga	Hold fast to your knowledge
Kia pua wai to moemoea	Your dreams will blossom
Kia kaha ra	Be strong, be strong
Kia kaha ra	Be strong, be strong

(written by Miriama Campbell)

Left: A loyal New Zealander, Michael has always displayed great pride in his Maori culture and heritage, and devotion to his family and friends. *Cambo Clothing*

55

There is no secret about what helps to drive Michael Campbell, professional golfer and currently the most visible Maori on the planet. His pride in his Maori culture is as plain to see as his brown face that lights up with an infectious, genuine smile. The New Zealander wore it for all the world to see when he won the 105th US Open at Pinehurst No 2.

Printed upon the back of his white polo shirt, running parallel to his spine and across his shoulder blades, was the Maori symbol mangopare, a hammerhead shark design which symbolises strength, determination and a never-give-up attitude. Like the hammerhead shark symbol, Campbell also took strength from the 'Kia Kaha Ra' song which is all about never giving up and following one's dreams. It's the nearest thing to a mission statement for Campbell, and it has stood him in good stead during a 12-year professional career that has had some resounding highs and some incredible lows.

The mangopare mantra has been a constant throughout the life and career of this proud and spiritual Maori with European ties back to Scotsman Sir Logan Campbell, a past mayor of Auckland.

Michael was born in Hawera, Taranaki, of Ngati Ruanui and Nga Rauru descent, the only son of Tom and Maria. He has a sister, Michelle, who, along with the extended Campbell whanau, has helped nourish and groom him for success. Campbell also received major support from his grandmother Titihuia when he was a young boy. When Campbell holed his final and winning putt at Pinehurst, he looked skyward and thanked his ancestors and family for the part they played.

Campbell's grandmother died when he was 16. They had shared a close bond and she had told him frequently that he would change people's lives.

'I know she's with me right now, and I'm sure when I holed that putt and looked to the sky I just thought to myself, she's there, smiling down on me with the rest of my ancestors,' Campbell told the world following his first Major win and first PGA Tour success in the United States. It hadn't come easy, but by staying determined and strong he had climbed a major sporting mountain.

Below: A pensive Campbell waits to putt on the 14th green during the third round of the 1995 Open Championship on the Old Course at St Andrews in Scotland. Michael burst into the world spotlight in this tournament, leading the field before finishing third.
J.D. Cuban/ALLSPORT

With this victory Campbell became the first come-from-behind winner at the US Open in seven years. He joined American Lee Janzen, who overhauled Payne Stewart in 1998. Campbell was the 57th player to make the US title his first Major victory and at that point he was the sixth first-time winner on the PGA Tour for 2005. He is now one of 23 international players to have won the 105-year-old title.

The win was his first in 63 starts in the United States and his best effort there since finishing runner-up in the 2002 Bay Hill Invitational. Significantly, it was the first win on the PGA Tour by a New Zealander since Craig Perks won The Players Championship in 2002. But, most notably, it was the first Major win by a Kiwi since Sir Bob Charles won The Open Championship 42 years earlier.

The win was life changing for Campbell and his family. He earned a five-year exemption on the PGA Tour and will be exempt from qualifying for the US Open for ten years. It also comes with five-year exemptions

to The Players Championship, The Masters, The Open Championship and The PGA Championship.

It is one of New Zealand's greatest sporting achievements and testament to someone who has held on to, and worked steadfastly towards, his dreams. Campbell is proof that determination, hard work and talent can combine for success, although he could have been excused for being distracted or dispirited during a golfing career which had, until then, promised much more than it had delivered.

There was a near-miss in the 1995 Open Championship, serious injury in 1996 and the pain of 18 consecutive missed cuts that followed. There was also a final nine-hole meltdown in the 2002 New Zealand Open that preceded a campaign notable for eight missed cuts in the United States.

But it's a career that turned a major corner in 2005 despite a horror start to his playing schedule.

When Campbell dumped his tee shot into water on the short par-4 7th at Gulf Harbour during February's Holden New Zealand Open, many Kiwis began to wonder. New Zealand's top-ranked golfer missed the cut in New Zealand's only major tournament for the second successive year. Three years earlier he'd talked it up at Middlemore and fell away as fellow Kiwi Mahal Pearce won.

When Sir Bob Charles played his last New Zealand Open in 2004 at The Grange, Campbell, like the first knight of Kiwi golf, missed the weekend play. That was a golfing jolt for most. The 2004 event was meant to be a celebration of Sir Bob's career and Kiwis had to watch then-amateur Brad Heaven carry the country's hopes before Australian journeyman Terry Price won.

The Gulf Harbour dunking and subsequent demise of Campbell highlighted a miserable 2005 home showing, the first time the event was co-sanctioned with the European Tour. New Zealand Golf chief executive Larry Graham said at the time the co-sanctioned event had raised the performance bar and it was up to New Zealand's golfers to lift themselves.

Right: Michael blasts a tee shot as part of the Longest Drive promotion for the Australian Open at Sydney Airport on 22 November 2004. The year was one of Campbell's worst, and included missing the cut at the New Zealand Open in February.
Mark Nolan/Getty Images

60

How far up the bar and how soon any could raise it wasn't known, but professionally the game and its Kiwi swingers appeared near rock bottom. The two best ranked — Campbell and David Smail — both missed the weekend, while Phil Tataurangi and Frank Nobilo were injured.

Greg Turner had hung up his clubs while Craig Perks and Grant Waite had their own struggles in America. Stephen Scahill and Steven Alker were left to fly the flag, finishing 17th and 7th respectively. Along with Gareth Paddison, they were the only three Kiwis to pass the halfway stage. Throw in the turmoil of 2004 when New Zealand Golf's chief executive Peter Dale and national coaches, led by Mal Tongue, resigned en masse and the Kiwi game hadn't been at a lower point for some time.

Smail had won the New Zealand Open in 2003 at The Grange. Campbell had won in 2000, beating Perks in sudden death at Wellington's Paraparaumu links, but since then the Wellingtonian had mainly struggled when the country's eyes focused each year on their big event.

His failures were inconceivable given his natural talent and the golfing public expected more. Don't be misled: Campbell expected more too — he just needed a way to find it.

Right: Winning on home turf. Michael sinks an eagle putt on the second play-off hole to beat fellow New Zealander Craig Perks in the 2000 New Zealand Open at Paraparaumu. The year was a good one for Campbell, with five key wins.
Nick Wilson/ALLSPORT

Michael Campbell has always been the drawcard for the home crowd. He has a charisma and swagger about him and he appeals to all Kiwis, from the struggling beneficiary to the wealthy high achiever. A strong family man, he has a boy-next-door charm coupled with a natural ability to relate to all people.

When he was home he would always talk the championship talk but many questioned whether he could indeed walk it. The situation wasn't helped by Campbell's criticism of the Gulf Harbour course when it was announced as the 2005 New Zealand Open venue late in 2004. His outburst — which was put down to an off-the-record conversation with a journalist finding its way into print — earned a censure from Australasian Tour chief executive Andrew Georgiou. They quickly kissed and made up with Campbell promoted as the poster boy in the build-up to the event won by Sweden's Niclas Fasth.

For the record, Campbell shot 73 and 70 at Gulf Harbour for a one-under-par total, and missed the cut by two shots, officially finishing tied for 101st.

To his enormous credit Campbell has appeared in every national Open, just as he'd promised former New Zealand Golf Association executive, the late Grant Clements. The administrator did much in the 1980s to establish the New Zealand academy system, of which Campbell was a part, and his annual appearance was his way of paying him back.

It's the one time of the year Campbell can come home, play in an event and spend time with his extended family — he has more than 65 first cousins — and friends. His New Zealand appearances were always the highlight for fans, while several other high-profile Kiwi professionals couldn't drag themselves Down Under.

After rising effortlessly to the professional ranks, Campbell won the Canon Challenge in just his fifth start in 1993. And despite winning 13 times worldwide prior to the US Open, the ranks of average Kiwi sports fans thirsting to see if Campbell, or any other New Zealander, could emulate Sir Bob Charles with a major success had thinned. Charles had never won the US Open, although he had twice finished third among his ten top-ten Major finishes, and it was in his sprig marks every other Kiwi golfer, including Campbell, trailed.

The knockers felt suitably justified for their negativity when Campbell missed his next three cuts after Auckland. That made five successive failures to start the year. The Heineken Classic, Holden New Zealand Open, Carlsberg Malaysian Open, Dubai Desert Classic and Qatar Masters respectively had all passed without Campbell firing a worthy challenge.

These tournament failures came on top of a horrible end to 2004 when Campbell shot consecutive closing rounds in the 80s during his final three appearances on the European Tour — at The Heritage, WGC American Express Championship and Volvo Masters Andalucia.

Many critics believed Campbell had officially lost it and the tournament placings seemed to back up that belief. These were the results of a player who had himself declared his golfing game was so foreign it was like aliens had invaded his body. He even thought about chopping up his clubs with an axe and giving the game away altogether in the late 1990s.

Not one of the doubters would have thought that, seven months later, Campbell — wearing the shiny new crowns of the US Open and World Match Play Championship — would be playing a major hand as the International team ran United States close in The Presidents Cup.

Left: Given his form and results of just a year earlier, Campbell fans could have been forgiven for not expecting too much of Michael at the US Open in 2005. But it was a different man walking the course. Here he lines up a putt on the 12th green during round two.
Jamie Squire/Getty Images

What people didn't know was that Campbell had started turning the corner early in 2005 and, while the results weren't immediately forthcoming, his solid golfing and mental foundation were beginning to take hold.

The technical basis had been grooved in his early years. First, as a junior at Wellington's Titahi Bay Golf Club, before he moved across to Manor Park and hooked up with swing guru Mal Tongue. He made his mark initially in Wellington golf and then worked his way into New Zealand sides. He became the first and only Kiwi to win the prestigious Australian Amateur Championship. He also combined with Phil Tataurangi, Stephen Scahill and Grant Moorhead to win the Eisenhower Trophy in 1992, before turning professional in 1993.

Right: A winning team: coach Jonathan Yarwood has been working full time with Michael Campbell since early 2005. *Golf World*

Far right: Silhouetted between towering pines, Michael tees off on the 11th hole during the final round of the US Open. No one has ever doubted Campbell's technical skills. Many commentators worldwide have admired his swing, and when in top form he makes it all look easy. *Ross Kinnaird/Getty Images*

Hours of practice and dreaming had seen him finally realise his childhood vision of becoming a professional golfer. But, 12 years on, he was still trying to find the way to becoming one of the best and deliver the results and standing to match his long-held desires.

He needed a change. Something to spark him up.

In early 2005 Campbell persuaded coach Jonathan Yarwood to move from his job at the David Leadbetter Golf Academy at Bradenton, Florida and come on board full-time to work with him. The reason was simply to help Campbell eradicate the dramatic fluctuations in form that had become synonymous with his career. When Campbell is on top of his game he makes it look very easy. His swing is pure and admired worldwide, but he has been prone to spasmodic rank shots and scoring blowouts.

Yarwood, who also works with Kiwi Stephen Scahill and Germany's Alex Cejka, remained based in Florida but freed himself to travel regularly to work with Campbell in Europe early in the year.

Campbell also took on a new sports psychologist in Nick Hastings, while long-time manager Andrew Ramsey departed on mutual terms and was replaced by IMG's global team, including Adrian Mitchell, Joanna Walkley and David Rollo.

Together, the cluster formed a new off-course combination that perfectly complemented the on-course working partnership and friendship Campbell had with regular caddie Michael Waite. Campbell and Waite, who began lugging bags in 1987, had already shared ten wins together prior to 2005.

Team Cambo had restructured and refocused. There were some slight changes in equipment: a new Callaway driver had been thrown into Campbell's bag earlier in the year with immediate gains. The Fusion FT3 didn't just add yardage and accuracy to Campbell's game, it also added confidence.

Confidence, a golfer's savoured 15th club, was needed to hit the shots and find the narrow fairways when Cambo attacked Pinehurst No 2 with the precision of a fairway surgeon.

Right: Onward to victory. The leaderboard tells the story as Campbell and caddie Michael Waite walk to the 18th green during the final round. The 'Fab Five' faltered, with Tiger Woods finishing two strokes behind, and Phil Mickelson, Ernie Els, Vijay Singh and Retief Goosen down or out.
Ross Kinnaird/Getty Images

70

And of course there was still one major player in this equation — Michael Campbell, the self-proclaimed 'just a Maori boy from Titahi Bay'. He was following his grandmother's direction; he was still believing, still determined and holding on to the dream of becoming the world's best golfer.

When Campbell arrived on the professional scene he was greeted as a superstar in the making. Former world number ones Greg Norman, Nick Faldo and Nick Price all talked of the special golfing talent Campbell possessed. They were all Major winners, and Campbell believers in the early years. Surely there was something in their early and lofty predictions?

With his new 2005 team on board, Campbell made steady progress in Europe. He gained top-ten finishes in the Johnnie Walker Classic, Daily Telegraph British Masters and BMW Championship. His last four-round tournament start in Europe prior to heading to the United States was a credible 15th in The Celtic Manor Wales Open.

When Campbell arrived at the US Open critics and fans alike still had no right to consider him among the favoured. He came with an 80th world ranking. It was improving — he'd fallen into the 100s and made the trip only after securing one of nine qualifying spots at Walton Heath Golf Club in England. It was the first time the USGA had held qualifying offshore.

Campbell made a late decision to play the qualifying tournament and because of that he and caddy Michael Waite would be at Pinehurst No 2 while wife Julie and sons Thomas and Jordan were back home in Brighton, England.

Not too many eyebrows would have been raised when Campbell arrived at the tournament venue. The American pre-tournament and daily focus was squarely on the 'Fab Five' of Tiger Woods, Phil Mickelson, Ernie Els, Vijay Singh and Retief Goosen. Could Woods win a second Major this year? Could Mickelson grab his second Major? Could Singh capture the first US Open for Fiji? Could Els win his third US Open? Could Retief Goosen

Right: Campbell has a light-hearted moment with runner-up Tiger Woods on the 18th green during the prize-giving ceremony after his US Open victory. On this day, Campbell showed he truly belonged in the company of the greats.
Ross Kinnaird/Getty Images

defend his title and join the select few to win three US Open titles in five years? Campbell was truly an underdog in this company and was offered as a 100–1 shot by the New Zealand TAB.

In New Zealand, the US Open build-up was a sideshow to the biggest sporting occasion since the America's Cup or when Tiger Woods graced these shores — the Lions versus All Blacks rugby. It was the first Lions tour since 1993, and in a rugby-mad country it justifiably took up most of the column inches and radio and television bulletins early in Open week.

That was until Monday 20 June, New Zealand time, when the country suddenly ground to a mid-morning halt. The reason was Campbell: after shooting a four-round even-par total, he would become the first New Zealander to win golf's toughest championship. En route to the title, he would outlast the game's greatest current player — Tiger Woods — and the remains of the 'Fab Five'.

Like many Kiwis, I had been following his progress throughout the tournament via television and the Internet. I have to admit I'd given him less than an even chance of making the cut at the beginning of the week. I knew of his record in the United States, and I'd heard him say he wasn't totally comfortable playing in that country. But I'd also seen him win at Paraparaumu and watched him flush hundreds of shots over the past decade. I too stayed up through the night in 1995 to watch him play The Open Championship — I was and am a Campbell fan. In my heart of hearts I harboured hope that something good could happen for him. He's a nice guy and has always swung the club like a champion.

Did I think he could win? No, not at that point, but I believed he could compete, and in the last round of a Major championship anything can happen. He just needed to be close and have a little bit of luck go his way for a top-five finish. No disgrace in that scenario, certainly a big improvement on his last four efforts at this tournament.

The *Chicago Tribune* gave him little chance, lumping him in with a bunch of no-hopers as a 'guy who was born in New Zealand into a Maori tribe ... who has missed the US Open cut four years in a row'.

The smart money was obviously on Goosen. The ice-cool South African had already proved he could get the job done in US Open conditions. And you couldn't discount Tiger, quite possibly the greatest player of all time and one with an impeccable sense of timing and occasion in Majors. And that was how many Kiwis felt heading into the final 36 holes.

Right: All the world's media eyes upon him. Campbell poses with the trophy for photographers after the US Open victory. Campbell's name is engraved alongside such legends of the game as Ben Hogan, Jack Nicklaus, Arnold Palmer, Payne Stewart and Tiger Woods.

David Cannon/Getty Images

Like many Kiwis on that Monday morning in New Zealand I watched it all unfold on television. The impact of Campbell and Waite inching towards the toughest of finishing lines was momentous, the effect on the country unbelievable. The New Zealand Government delayed its Cabinet meeting to crowd around televisions, workers around the country found excuses to find televisions or radios while a hearty group, including Michael's immediate family, took it all in, appropriately, at the Titahi Bay Golf Club.

Above: Post-US Open was a whirlwind
few weeks for Michael and family
of photocalls, travel and celebration
before coming back to earth. Not far
from their home in Brighton, Campbell
and his wife, Julie, show off the
winner's trophy in sedate surf.
Julian Herbert/Getty Images

Prime Minister Helen Clark labelled Campbell's win as stunning. 'His win is a triumph of immense skill, determination and perseverance, along with great modesty and humility.' It was, she said, one of New Zealand's greatest sporting achievements and cemented Campbell's place as one of New Zealand's sporting greats.

Campbell stopped the country in its tracks, and at least two staunch supporters, separated by thousands of kilometres but linked by television, wept. Vic Pirihi, a retired real-estate businessman, and Jamie Kupa, golf professional, were going about their business with Ngaki Tamariki Trust. The Auckland-based organisation helps mainly young Maori play golf and Campbell and Phil Tataurangi are its inspirational ambassadors. Pirihi was in an American restaurant on the way to Canada with top amateurs Brad Iles, Doug Holloway and Riki Kauika. None of them left their vantage points until the final putt dropped.

Pirihi had been one of Campbell's early sounding boards. They had played each other in Maori golf tournaments and Pirihi had helped knock some of the rough edges off the teenaged Campbell. Those now-distant traits included long hair, an earring and a typical teenage know-it-all attitude.

Kupa was alone in an Australian motel, finishing his time on a Prime Minister's Scholarship, and was glued to every shot.

When Campbell rolled in the two-foot bogey putt for a two-stroke win over Woods both men cried tears of joy, accomplishment and pride. Their emotional outpouring came from years of being involved with Campbell on the way to his win. Along with Campbell's family, Pirihi and Kupa knew just what he had done to get this far and they were filled with satisfaction.

'I wept, I was so proud ... to have known him so long, to see where he's come from,' said Kupa. 'We have all the steps covered — New Zealand Amateur, North Island, South Island, club champions ... and now a Major winner.

'We sow the seed early. Now we have one at the top of the mountain; it just happens he has a brown face and a flat nose.'

It wasn't just any New Zealander holding aloft the trophy. It was Campbell, a proud Maori and an incredible New Zealand role model gripping the most sought after golfing trophy in the United States; a trophy which golfing greats Sir Bob Charles, Sam Snead, Greg Norman and Vijay Singh hadn't secured but one on which legendary names like Ben Hogan, Jack Nicklaus, Arnold Palmer, Payne Stewart, Tiger Woods and now Michael Campbell were etched.

Hogan had been a hero of Campbell's since he was a young boy and the thought of having his name on the same trophy had his mind in a whirl at the post-tournament interview.

'I can see his name on here four times ... and mine's going to be down there somewhere. It's just a — Arnold Palmer, Jack Nicklaus — sorry guys, I'm just diverging here. Oh man, it's just unbelievable; that's all I can say,' Campbell strung together for the world's press.

Campbell, much to his pleasure, had knocked Tana Umaga and the boys in black off the front and leading sports pages.

Michael Campbell had stood tall during a ferocious test of golf, finishing even par from his four rounds, and displaying a calmness and assuredness that only the world's best show under the competition blowtorch. It was the highest winning total since 1998 when Janzen also scored 280 to win at the Olympic Club in San Francisco.

Right: Party time at the Campbell home in Brighton, England, as Michael and Julie joined family and friends on Sunday 26 June to celebrate the US Open victory.

As *The New Zealand Herald* editorialised the following day, Campbell had gone from oblivion to the top of the golfing world. And New Zealand and Larry Graham loved it as the country officially went Michael Campbell and golf mad. The New Zealand Golf chief executive saw an opportunity to cash in big-time. Graham said the win was a great advertisement for New Zealand and perfect timing as he sought to get government and major sponsorship for future New Zealand Open tournaments.

Left: He answered the call and now he can bring the trophy home. A large and happy crowd cheered with delight as Michael raised the silverware on arrival at Auckland International Airport on 27 July, at the start of a busy celebratory tour.
Phil Walter/Getty Images

'We want to give New Zealanders the chance to see the best golfers in the world,' he was quoted as saying.

In the eyes of the United States at least, Campbell's win was greeted with the same manner as Ben Curtis winning the 2003 Open Championship. Another golfing unknown getting in the way of the best players, some said. In fact, most of the Stateside after-match comment centred around why Tiger Woods didn't win as opposed to Campbell's fine play on one of the most difficult courses in the world against the world's best players.

Given Campbell's rollercoaster career, it's not hard to imagine that if he was an American a movie of his story would be swiftly in the works. Sure, there was an appearance on the *Late Show with David Letterman* but one got the sense the United States commentators were more intrigued with Campbell than paying him an appropriate sporting tribute.

Campbell handled it all with dignity and appeared at ease when put under the spotlight. Understandably and justifiably, the reaction was very different in New Zealand. Callaway Golf took out sizeable ads in newspapers and magazines. Campbell was, after all, their first male Major winner, obtained with the new Fusion FT3 driver, which he unashamedly said put yards and accuracy into his bag.

Right: The Campbells' tour began at Auckland International Airport with a powhiri, a traditional Maori challenge and welcome. With Michael are his wife, Julie, and two sons, Jordan and Thomas (right). Phil Walter/Getty Images

New Zealand's Prime Minister had been an observer of Campbell's career since his emergence as an amateur in the Eisenhower Cup-winning quartet.

'We have watched his highs and lows and we have watched him in more troubled times. Nobody deserves such an immense victory more than Michael,' she said.

Sport and Recreation Minister Trevor Mallard also joined the well-wishing.

'It's great to see Michael hung in there ... It's a testament to not only his skills as a golfer but also his dedication and commitment that see him reaching a pinnacle of his sport today.'

The excited and distracted Cabinet didn't head back into business until Campbell held aloft the impressive glistening trophy.

By this time the party was in full steam at Titahi Bay with a proud Thomas (Tom) Campbell receiving the best Father's Day present possible from his son (in the US, Father's day falls in June). The pair had talked the previous day and Tom told Rotorua's *Daily Post* his son was full of confidence heading into the final round.

'I was a nervous wreck watching the round ... This has always been his dream. As an 11 and 12 year old he always dreamed of being the world's best golfer. Now he is,' Tom said proudly.

Above: Taking it to the top. Campbell shows his trophy to long-time fan, New Zealand Prime Minister Helen Clark at Parliament in Wellington, on 2 August. Clark said: 'We have watched his highs and lows and we have watched him in more troubled times. Nobody deserves such an immense victory more than Michael.'
Ross Setford/Getty Images

Above: A proud supporter of the All Blacks, Campbell got the chance to share his victory with captain Tana Umaga and the team during All Black training at Trust Park, Waitakere, Auckland on 28 July.
Ross Land/Getty Images

Opposite: Campbell's win stopped the country in its tracks and suddenly we had a new champion and hero. The reception Michael received in his home region was tremendous, and he reciprocated with numerous engagements and talks to fans and well-wishers, including these school children at Titahi Bay on 29 July.
Ross Setford/Getty Images

The party would continue through to late July when the newly crowned US Open Champion, his family and the trophy would return to New Zealand for ten days of celebration. It was hot on the heels of Campbell finishing fifth at The Open Championship, proving to many that Pinehurst was no fluke, and that his game had simply reached another level.

About 300 people greeted Cambo and family at Auckland International Airport, creating a commotion for the troglodytes who didn't know the significance of the fanfare. A conference had been coordinated by IMG and New Zealand Golf to satisfy the hordes of media wanting to finally talk to the champ after chasing family, friends, former coaches and teammates for stories.

True to his simple roots, after his Auckland commitments Campbell spent the night with family. They reportedly enjoyed a home-cooked meal of roast lamb before heading home to Wellington the next day.

Campbell said he'd been blown away by the greeting in Auckland and in New Zealand's capital city the reaction was about to floor the unflappable champion. Some 125,000 people were there to welcome him. It was humbling and inspiring for the sportsman and his family. They were honoured with a ticker-tape parade and a civic reception in the city before attending another in Titahi Bay, about 15 kilometres from Wellington.

It was announced that a street would be named after him in his hometown. It was a time of unashamed patriotism and backslapping with speeches and presentations galore. Children swarmed to Campbell, inspired by his efforts. Golf was once again on everyone's lips.

Campbell was a returning hero, joining famous Kiwis like Ernest, Lord Rutherford, Sir Edmund Hillary, Sir Bob Charles, Peter Snell and Sir Peter Blake who had contributed to not only New Zealand but world history.

The spin-off for New Zealand was in obvious exposure, with Campbell proud to call the Land of the Long White Cloud his home. His Open win followed New Zealand resort courses Cape Kidnappers and Kauri Cliffs (where Michael is the touring professional) being judged among the world's best.

Right: His name is indelibly etched on the US Open trophy and he has also left his mark in Wellington. Campbell holds aloft the sign of a street named in his honour at a welcome reception at Porirua City, on 29 July. 'Drive' is obviously more appropriate for a golfer than 'Street'.
Ross Setford/Getty Images

There was also an unexpected windfall from one of Campbell's earliest supporters. One of his first sponsors, AMP, had dug out Campbell's old contract and realised they had pledged him a $10,000 bonus if he won the US Open. Despite the agreement being well and truly expired, the company, which has supported New Zealand junior and senior golf for many years, handed Campbell the cheque. He didn't hold it for long, passing it on to New Zealand Golf to help with its junior programme.

Campbell wants to leave a legacy to New Zealand golf and he is well on his way to doing that through his donations and inspiration. The gesture continued Campbell's legacy of donating his tournament earnings in New Zealand and from the 2005 Presidents Cup to charity. He and wife Julie have regularly contributed to Ronald McDonald House in Wellington since 1995.

One of the biggest understatements in the wake of Campbell's success was the possibility of his future earnings. Former Kiwi touring professional Greg Turner said at the time of Campbell's US Open win that the potential was there for him to multiply his $1.65 million winnings by at least five if he could retain his form.

There was obvious calculation and slight reservation in that statement, more than likely attributed to Campbell's past career. It was possible a dip in form could come. Many a good player has lost focus after securing one of golf's most coveted prizes.

But Campbell was in a new place, surrounded by his people and oozing confidence. He also had plenty of bad, and now good, golfing experiences on which to draw. Technically, his game was tight and mentally he was in tune.

By October he had well and truly cemented himself among the world's best and highest-earning players. His form was top drawer and he followed up his Major showings, finishing tied for sixth in the last of the year's Majors, the US PGA at Baltusrol, by taking out the World Match Play Championship. That prestigious title came with a £1 million winner's cheque after he beat Irishman Paul McGinley 2 and 1 in the final. The high-flying Campbell joined Sir Bob Charles as the only Kiwi winners of that title.

He also anchored the International team in their narrow 18.5 to 15.5 loss to the United States in The Presidents Cup and improved his world ranking to 16th. Campbell is now well on his way to his career goal of being 'the best golfer to have come out of New Zealand'. It's a title Sir Bob Charles and many other Kiwis would proudly see Campbell wear.

And next June, Campbell will be called to the tee at the majestic Winged Foot Golf Club in Mamaroneck, New York as the defending US Open champion. He will be the first Kiwi to receive that honour and the first golfer from Australasia since Aussie David Graham won in 1981.

Not bad for 'just a Maori boy from Titahi Bay'.

**Above: Campbell continued his
superb form shown in the US Open
by taking out the World Match
Play title at Wentworth on 18
September, beating Irishman Paul
McGinley 2 and 1 in the final. He
receives well-deserved hugs from
Jordan and Thomas.**
Odd Andersen/AFP/Getty Images

Michael Campbell's winning road to Pinehurst

Amateur

1992   Australian Amateur Championship
        Eisenhower Trophy

Professional

1993   Canon Challenge
1994   Memorial Olivier Barras
        Bank Austria Open
        Audi Quattro Trophy
1995   Alfred Dunhill Masters

2000   Crown Lager New Zealand Open
        Ericsson Masters
        Johnnie Walker Classic
        Heineken Classic
        Linde German Masters
2001   Heineken Classic
2002   Smurfit European Open
2003   Nissan Irish Open
2005   US Open Championship

Contributors' notes

Michael Campbell was born in Hawera in 1969 and grew up in Titahi Bay, north of Wellington. Since turning professional in 1993 he has won 15 tournaments, culminating in the 2005 US Open Championship and World Match Play Championship. He and his family live in Brighton, England. Michael maintains strong links with New Zealand, including generous support for junior golf and charities.

Sir Bob Charles is New Zealand's most successful golfer, with a professional career spanning more than four decades. His victory in The Open Championship in 1963 was the only Major tournament win by a Kiwi golfer until Michael Campbell's exploits in 2005.

Martin Crowe is best known as one of New Zealand's greatest cricketers, and captained the national team from 1990 to 1993. Now Executive Producer, Cricket with Sky Network Television in Auckland, he is a passionate golfer and fan who was present at the 2005 US Open.

Craig Tiriana is sports editor of *The Daily Post* newspaper in Rotorua. Named New Zealand golf journalist of the year for 2003, he specialises in golf, cricket, rugby league and triathlon writing, and plays golf off a 2 handicap.